**This book ~~belongs to:~~**
*is shared with*

Sophie
Paterson

Mum Dad

# the prayer who searched for God

to all who pray

© 2016 Conscious Stories LLC

Illustrations by Alexis Aronson

Published by
Conscious Stories LLC
4800 Baseline Rd,
Suite E104-365
Boulder, CO
80303
USA

www.consciousstories.com

First Edition
Library of Congress
Control Number: 2017901961
ISBN 978-1-943750-06-1

Printed in China

1 2 3 4 5 6 7 8 9 10

**The last 20 minutes of every day are precious.**

# Dear parents, teachers, and readers,

This story has been gift-wrapped with two simple mindfulness practices to help you connect more deeply with your children in the last 20 minutes of each day.

● Quietly set your intention for calm and open connection.

● Then start your story time with the **Snuggle Breathing Meditation**. Read each line aloud and take slow, deep breaths together in order to relax and be present.

● At the end of the story, you can **Breathe Your Prayers**. This will help your children to grow their curiosity and awareness of breath and prayer. This simple activity will help them connect from deep in their hearts to the loving presence of God.

Enjoy snuggling into togetherness!

Andrew

## An easy breathing meditation

# Snuggle Breathing

Our story begins with us breathing together.
Say each line aloud and then
take a slow deep breath in and out.

I breathe for me

I breathe for you

I breathe for us

I breathe for all that surrounds us

Once upon a time,
there was a prayer
who went searching for God.

She left the heart that
yearned her into being,
jumping onto a breath
as it left the lips that spoke
her into being.

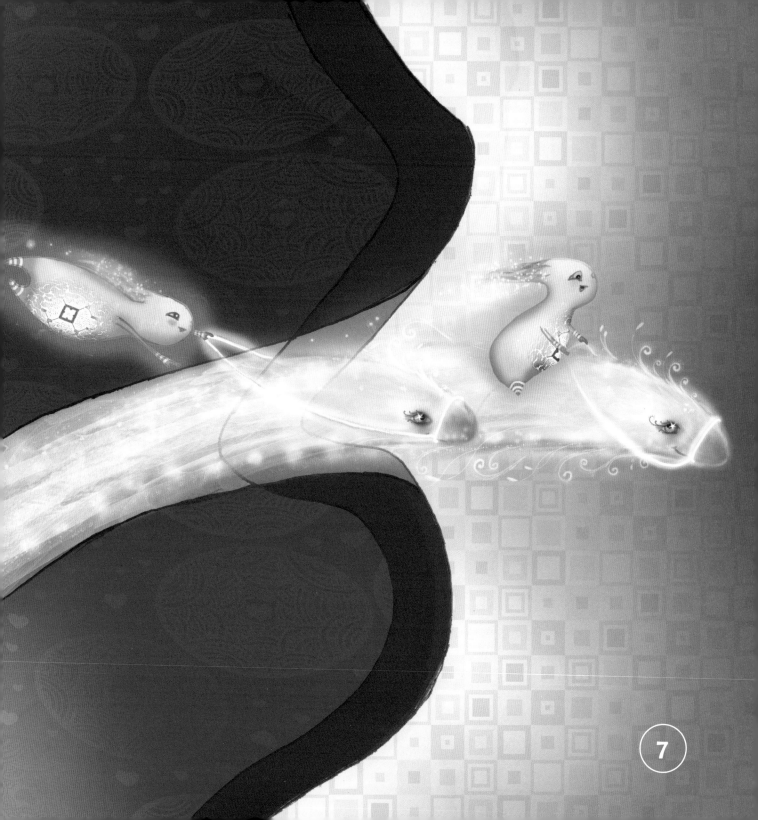

Out and away she flew,
searching for God.

She had heard that heaven was high above the sky, so she flew there first.

10

In the blink of an eye
she passed the clouds
and passed the moon
and passed the stars,

but she couldn't find God.

11

She remembered the sacred places
where people prayed to God,
so she turned the breath to visit them.

She flew over domes and spires,
weaving through the rooftops.

She still couldn't find God.

She asked the breath to turn again.

This time she flew through the seas
and the soils,
searching the earth.

14

Still she couldn't find God.

The breath paused.
It could go no further.

It was time to return home.

The prayer clung on tight
as the breath rushed home,
past the seas and soils,
past the sacred places,

past the stars,
past the moon, and
past the clouds,

20

back through the lips that
spoke her into being.

Right there,
in the narrow passage of the lips
where the breath rushed the fastest,
tickling the tongue...

there she found God,

quietly whispering,

# I am everywhere.

> **If the only prayer you ever say in your entire life is thank you, it will be enough.**
>
> **— Eckhart Tolle**

Have you said thank you for your day?

Have fun feeling each breath and prayer as you send them out into the world and breathe them back home to yourself.

## A simple way to pray

# Breathe Your Prayers

Can you feel your breath passing over your lips as you breathe in?

Can you feel your breath passing over your lips as you breathe out?

Is there a special prayer of thanks that wants to jump onto your next breath?

Silently breathe
out the words
"Thank you."
Feel your lips
tingle.

**4**

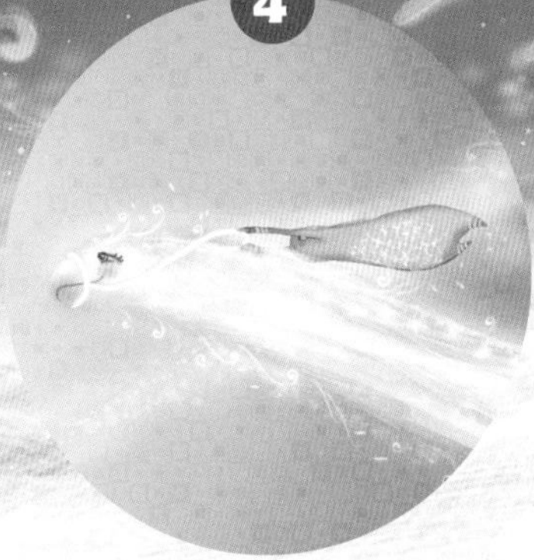

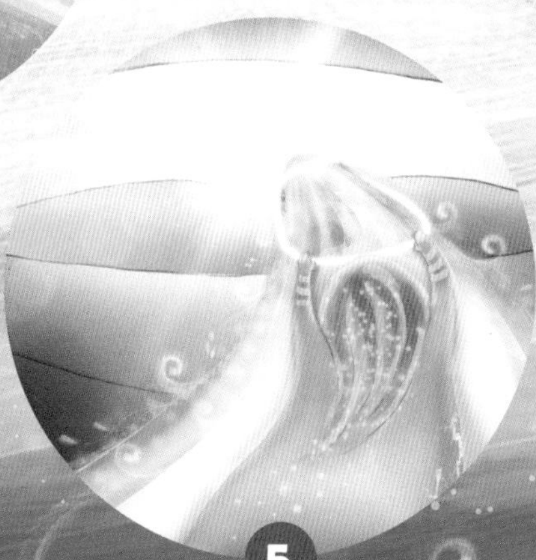

Do any other prayers want
to ride a breath before
sleep? You can send
them now.

**6**

Sleep tight.

**7**

**5**

Silently breathe in
the words "Thank
you." Feel your
tongue tickle.

the collection

The Conscious Bedtime Story Club

*snuggling into togetherness*

the prayer who searched for God

Andrew Newman

the fish who searched for water

the bee who could not choose her flower

Andrew Newman

the dad who didn't know

the hug who got stuck

Andre

the forgetful elephant

Andrew Newman

the laughing witch

Andrew Newman

a little light

Andrew Newman

the elephant who tried to tiptoe

how diablo became Spirit

Andrew Newman & Anna Breytenbach

the tree of goodness

Andrew Newman

the boy who searched for silence

Andrew Newman

# what the club offers

A collection of stories with wise and lovable characters who teach spiritual values to your children

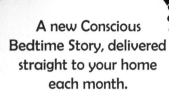

A new Conscious Bedtime Story, delivered straight to your home each month.

The Conscious Bedtime Story Club
*snuggling into togetherness*

## One whole year of bedtime stories

Meet wonderful, heroic characters with big hearts and deep values as they encounter exciting challenges and move toward freedom.

## Simple mindfulness practices

Enjoy easy breathing practices that soften the atmosphere and create deep connection when reading together.

## Create your own story books

Unleash your creativity by writing and coloring your own stories.

## Reflective activity pages

Cherish open sharing time with your children at the end of each day.

## Delivered to your home

Make one decision today, and experience a whole year of delightful stories.

## Supportive parenting community

Join a community of conscious parents who seek connection with their children.

## Download your free coloring book from
## www.consciousstories.com

## Andrew Newman - author

Andrew Newman has followed his deep longing for connection and his passion for spiritual development in a 12 year-long study of healing. He is a graduate of the Barbara Brennan School of Healing and a qualified Non-dual Kabbalistic healer. He has been actively involved in men's work through the Mankind Project since 2006.

In addition to his therapy practice, Andrew has published over 1,500 donated poems as the PoemCatcher, served as a volunteer coordinator for Habitat for Humanity in South Africa, and directed Edinburgh's Festival of Spirituality and Peace.

## Alexis Aronson — illustrator

Alexis is a self taught illustrator, designer and artist, currently working from Cape Town, South Africa. She has a passion for serving projects with a visionary twist that incorporates image making with the growth of human consciousness for broader impact.

Her media ranges from digital illustration and design to fine art techniques, such as intaglio printmaking, ceramic sculpture, and painting. In between working for clients and creating her own art for exhibition, Alexis is an avid nature lover, swimmer, yogi, hiker, and gardener.

www.alexisaronson.com

**stickers
for
sharing**
and for your
Star Counter

# Star Counter

Every time you breathe together and read aloud, you make a star shine in the night sky.

Place a sticker, or color in a star, to count how many times you have read this book.